JOURNAL

PETER PAUPER PRESS, INC.
WHITE PLAINS, NEW YORK

Cover illustration by David Cole Wheeler

Copyright © 2012
Peter Pauper Press, Inc.
202 Mamaroneck Avenue
White Plains, NY 10601
All rights reserved
ISBN 978-1-4413-0804-7
Printed in China
7 6 5 4 3 2 1

Visit us at www.peterpauper.com